Awareness of Language

Comparing Languages

English and its European relatives

Jim McGurn

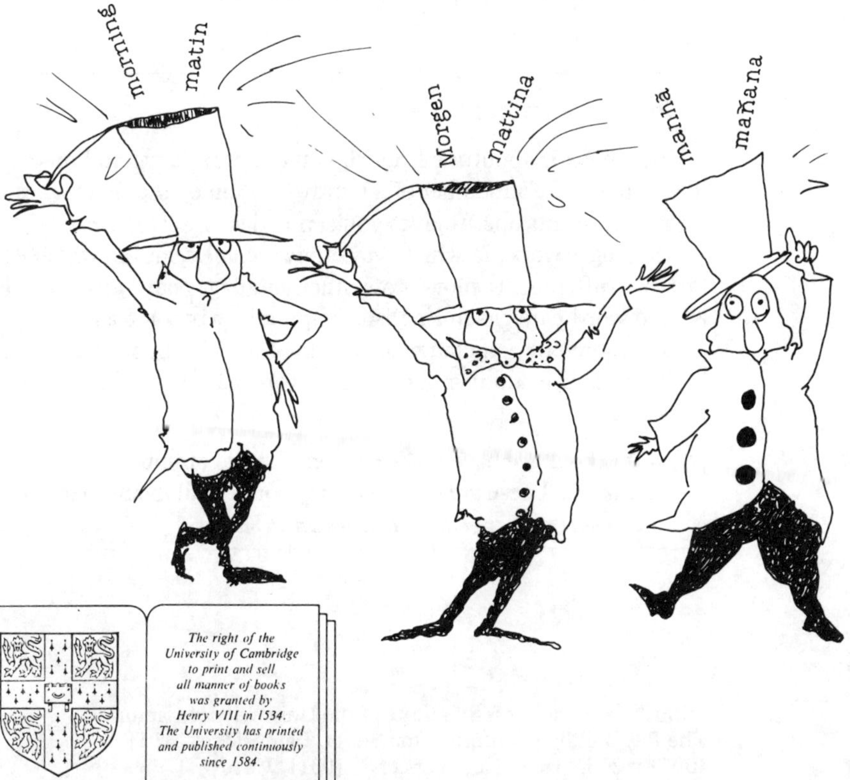

CAMBRIDGE UNIVERSITY PRESS

Cambridge
New York   Port Chester
Melbourne   Sydney

Awareness of Language

Series Editor: Eric Hawkins

The *Awareness of Language* series is an introduction to how language works which will be useful in the context of Modern Languages and/or English teaching. This book is one of several short topic books, each of which covers a particular aspect of language – with a strong emphasis on practical activities involving the pupil. The books may be used one at a time, in any order – together they form a coherent whole covering the main aspects of language awareness.

From the author

This book is about the English you use every day and how it is related – like a member of a family – to some other languages spoken in Europe. It gives you some idea of how these languages work, in which ways they are alike, and in which ways different. It shows how other languages have given words and word patterns to English, helping it to become a richer and more powerful language for all of us. The book also shows how English and its relatives in Europe have spread across the world.

In this book we have made no mention of community languages. These are dealt with in more detail in another book in this series, *Language Varieties and Change*.

Published by the Press Syndicate of the University of Cambridge
The Pitt Building, Trumpington Street, Cambridge CB2 1RP
40 West 20th Street, New York, NY 10011, USA
10 Stamford Road, Oakleigh, Melbourne, 3166, Australia

© Cambridge University Press 1991

First published 1991

Printed in Great Britain by GreenShires Print Ltd, Kettering

ISBN 0 521 33638 4

DS

Contents

1. Why compare languages?
2. How they got there
3. A language map
4. The sounds we make
5. Writing the sounds down
6. Dutch
7. German
8. Swedish
9. Italian
10. Spanish
11. French
12. How do languages compare?
13. How English links up
14. Last but not least

Symbols

The book provides a wide variety of activities, marked as follows:

S	for pupils working alone (solo)
P	to be done with a partner
G	for group work

Cassette

The cassette is strongly recommended. It has been specially produced to serve as a guide to the pronunciation of the languages met in this book. It also offers simple transcription exercises for pupils to practise their listening skills. On the cassette liner is a list of IPA symbols with examples from all the languages; this can be freely photocopied.

Cassette   0 521 33486 1
Book   0 521 33638 4

1 Why compare languages?

Look at a map of Europe. Imagine that you are touring round and need to buy food. In a Swedish shop you might hear words like *bröd* (bread), *mjölk* (milk) and *dyr* (dear, expensive). In Germany it would be *Brot, Milch* and *teuer*. In the Netherlands you would hear Dutch: *brood, melk* and *duur*. In France: *pain, lait* and *cher*. In Spain you would hear *pan, leche* and *caro*, and in Italy: *pane, latte* and *caro*.

You may have guessed from this that there are relationships between these languages. In fact, they all belong (together with English) to the great family of languages known as Indo-European. The languages on the left are from other parts of the same family. Find out where each is spoken, and look the places up in an atlas.

Greek
Czech
Russian
Punjabi
Welsh
Breton
Nepali

There are other great language families in the world. There is, for example, the Chinese–Tibetan family, and the Semitic family containing Arabic and Hebrew.

This book compares six European languages (Dutch, German, Swedish, Italian, Spanish and French) and relates them to English. This will help you to understand how the English language you use grew out of contact between two European branches of the Indo-European language family. Comparing these languages with English may help you appreciate some things about English (spellings that seem strange at first, or the way English grammar works) that you may not have thought much about until now. It may also help you discover how the foreign language you may be studying in school fits into the language map of Europe.

2 How they got there

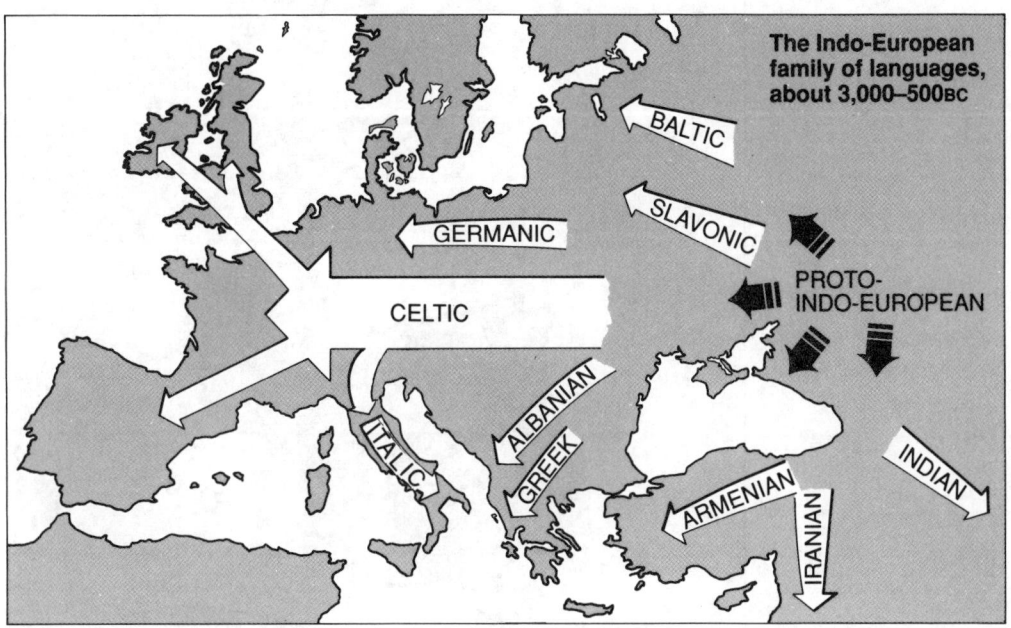

All the Indo-European languages are descended from a language (which scholars call Proto-Indo-European) of which we have no direct knowledge, but which is generally thought to have been spoken by tribes living somewhere to the east of Europe about 5,000 years ago. Gradually these tribes split up. Some moved eastwards into India, and others moved westwards. Their languages changed, and became different from one another, but each kept words and ways of using them which had been passed on from the Indo-European mother language. One group of Indo-European tribes, the Celts, became particularly powerful. About 500 years BC their territory stretched over much of Europe, including the British Isles.

The spead of Latin from about 100BC–400AD

About 300 years BC the area round the Mediterranean Sea was a great centre of activity. A huge Greek empire rose and fell. Then a new empire, centred on Rome, began to spread outwards from Italy. This Roman Empire was to last over 700 years. Its language, Latin, later developed into the ROMANCE languages: Italian, Spanish, French, and others.

As the Roman Empire lost strength, various Germanic tribes became more active. The language of the North Germanic tribes developed into today's Danish, Swedish, Norwegian and Icelandic. The language of the West Germanic tribes developed into modern German and Dutch – and also Frisian, a language spoken on the Dutch coast.

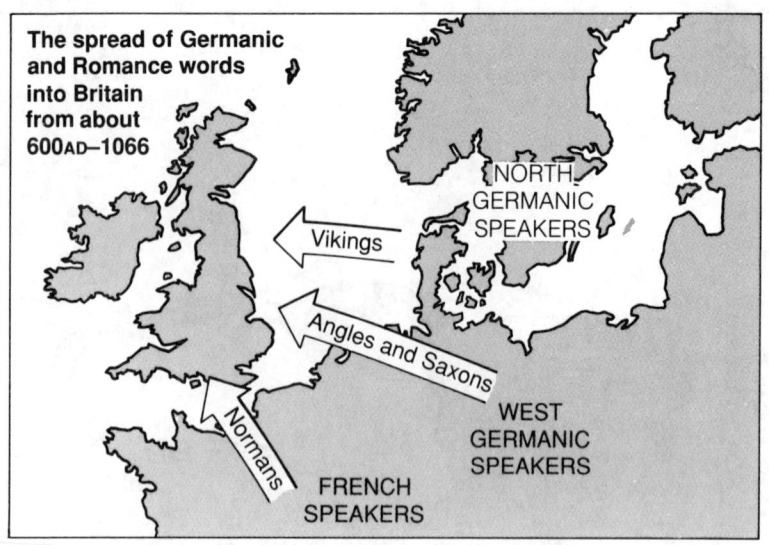

How did all this movement of tribes affect what people spoke in Britain? The Angles, Saxons and other tribes invaded England, where they were well settled by 600 AD. They brought with them West Germanic words. Then came Viking invaders, from the 800s onwards, bringing their North Germanic words into English. Next, in 1066, came the Norman invasion from France, bringing many thousands of Romance words to the Germanic core of English.

The Indo-European languages, like all living languages, have kept on changing. Traders, travellers, priests, seamen and

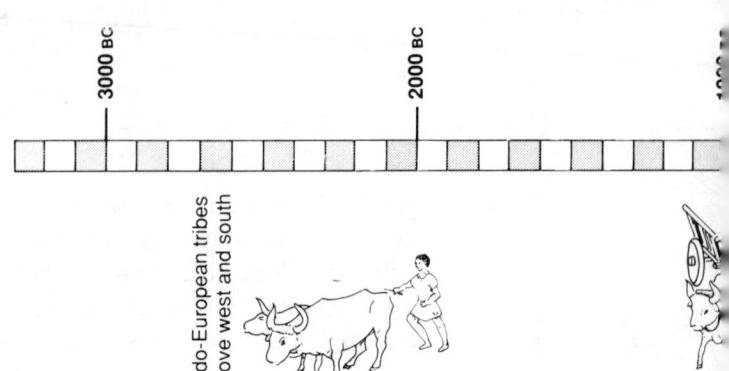

soldiers moved around Europe, spreading new words, names and ideas from one language to another. Languages are still on the move, but are also affected by newer developments. Give examples of how each of these might bring people into closer contact with other languages.

television   record players   better transport
schools for everyone   multinational companies

Before there were trains and cars and planes, people stayed put. So each group had to make up their own language. They didn't need to bother about anybody else understanding them. That's why each language is completely different from any other...

Television is becoming more and more international. A Belgian girl in Ghent can switch on a Dutch language channel for the news, then switch to a French channel for a pop concert from Paris. Then she might watch an Italian film broadcast on German television, or she might prefer one of the international satellite channels. People who watch television in other languages can pick up words and phrases to use in their own language.

Over half the people in the world speak more than one language. However, there are still many in Europe who know only their mother tongue. So notices and printed materials are often put into several languages. This is particularly important when a product is meant to be sold in perhaps five or six countries. Find two food packets with the writing in several languages, and try to work out which language is which. Find a clothing label with sizes and washing instructions in two languages and compare them. You can make a multi-language folder or wall display from labels and empty packets.

Put Superbrain right. Use examples from the language maps to back up your arguments.

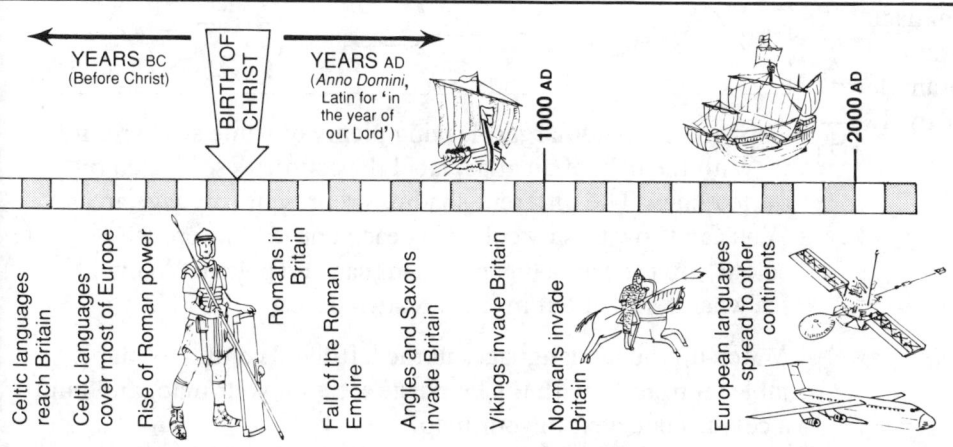

3 A language map

Each country has its own separate language, right? What do they speak in Portugal? Portuguese! And in Switzerland? Swiss, of course. And your Austrians aren't going to speak German, are they? And English is only spoken in...

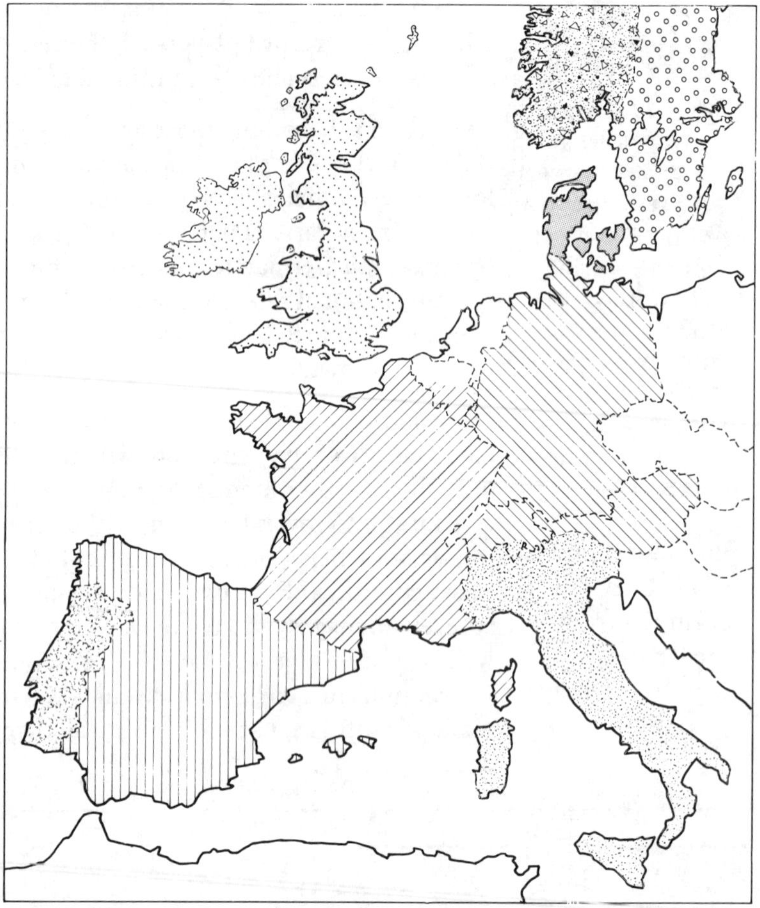

Use the information from your language map to take Superbrain down a peg or two!

[S] ' Copy this map out larger, leaving plenty of white space round it. With the help of an atlas, label the countries separated by dotted lines. The different shadings represent language areas. (You can show this by colouring each one in a different colour.) In each area one main language is spoken. You will see what it's all about in the next two pages.

Match up the ten languages in the left-hand column of the table on page 11 with the language areas on your map, and put a colour-code next to your map.

If you glance down each word list below you will notice links between these languages (remember the food shop words). There are two branches in this group of Indo-European languages. By looking closely at the features of the words in each column, decide which six languages belong to one branch of the family, and which four to the other. Then draw a long line on your map to divide one branch from the other.

DANISH	ny	syv	koge	morgen	salt
DUTCH	nieuw	zeven	koken	morgen	zout
ENGLISH	new	seven	to cook	morning	salt
FRENCH	nouveau	sept	cuire	matin	sel
GERMAN	neu	sieben	kochen	Morgen	Salz
ITALIAN	nuovo	sette	cucinare	mattina	sale
NORWEGIAN	ny	syv/sju	koke/koka	morgen	salt
PORTUGUESE	novo	sete	cozinhar	manhã	sal
SPANISH	nuevo	siete	cocinar	mañana	sal
SWEDISH	ny	sju	koka	morgon	salt

Your dividing line on the map separates the Romance languages from the Germanic ones. (Look again at pages 6, 7 and 8). Your map does not show all the languages in these groups. There is Rumanian, for example, in the Romance group, and Icelandic in the Germanic.

Sometimes you find one set of similar words in the Romance languages, and a completely different set of corresponding words in the Germanic languages. English often links up with both sets:

ROMANCE: ITALIAN bottiglia
SPANISH botella
FRENCH bouteille

} ENGLISH bottle/flask

GERMANIC: DUTCH fles
GERMAN Flasche
SWEDISH flaska

11

Think of words in English related to the two parts of each of these lists:

ITALIAN	luna	terra	timido	aiutare	cantare
SPANISH	luna	tierra	tímido	ayudar	cantar
FRENCH	lune	terre	timide	aider	chanter
DUTCH	maan	aarde	schuw	helpen	zingen
GERMAN	Mond	Erde	scheu	helfen	singen
SWEDISH	måne	jord	skygg	hjälpa	sjunga

4 The sounds we make

The languages of Western Europe all use some sounds which you don't hear in English. You pronounce them by making your mouth do things it is not used to doing. In a similar way, sounds such as our *r* in *ring* and *th* in *the* need to be specially practised by foreign children learning English.

On the cassette are speakers from other parts of Europe, speaking English. Speech habits from their own language show through. They're not too worried about it; the main thing is that they are getting their message across.

DUTCH	SPANISH
een	uno
twee	dos
drie	tres
vier	cuatro
vijf	cinco
zes	seis
zeven	siete
acht	ocho
negen	nueve
tien	diez

Try this little test. On the left are the numbers one to ten in Dutch. Have a go at saying them out loud.

Now listen to the Dutch speaker on the cassette reading the same numbers. Try to imitate exactly what you hear. Compare the sounds with what you guessed they might be. Do the same with the numbers in Spanish.

The words below mean *rich*. Say each one exactly as you hear it:

DUTCH *rijk*   GERMAN *reich*   SWEDISH *rik*

ITALIAN *ricco*   SPANISH *rico*   FRENCH *riche*

Are the *r* sounds all the same, and how do they compare with the way YOU pronounce the *r* in English *rich*?

ENGLISH	gray, giant, gnome
DUTCH	grijs
SWEDISH	grå, gäst
GERMAN	grau, Montag, hungrig
ITALIAN	grigio, gigante, gnomo
SPANISH	gris, gigante
FRENCH	gris, géant

Listen to these words and imitate them. How many different sounds represented by *g* can you spot?

Even though all these languages use the same Roman (ABC) alphabet, the Roman letters are pronounced differently in each language.

However, there is a way of showing in WRITING the sounds of any language. You can do this using the special signs of the International Phonetic Alphabet (IPA), which was invented in the 1890s. Each IPA sign matches a given sound, no matter which language is being written. The Dutch word *hond* (English: *dog*) ends, when it is spoken, with a *t* sound. So the IPA spelling is [hont]. IPA spellings are put in square brackets to stop you mixing them up with normal spellings.

Many of the IPA signs look and behave like English letters. Others look very different, and for good reasons. Say *this* and *thin*. You use your voice for the *th* of *this*, but not for the *th* of *thin*. So two different phonetic signs are needed: you write [ð is] and [θ in].

For more on IPA and how to say the foreign words in this book, see the cassette and its liner.

13

Stresses and tunes

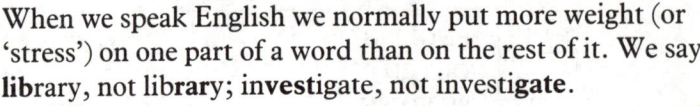

When we speak English we normally put more weight (or 'stress') on one part of a word than on the rest of it. We say **lib**rary, not lib**rary**; in**ves**tigate, not investi**gate**.

When we speak we harmonise these stresses with another form of stress which has to do with the rhythm of the sentence as a whole. Say this out loud:
I've decided to have a party on Friday.

You probably put quite a lot of stress on certain syllables:
I've decided to have a **par**ty on **Fri**day.

The syllables stressed come in the words to which the speaker draws attention. They also form part of a regular beat in the language. So, to keep this beat going we often quicken up through the 'unimportant' unstressed syllables between stresses.

The French, on the other hand, say all their syllables at a fairly steady rate: the more there are, the longer it takes to say them. (French does have stresses, roughly on every other syllable, but they are weaker, and are fixed more to individual words rather than to the overall meaning of a sentence.)

Roughly speaking, the Romance languages (French, Italian, Spanish, etc.) are 'syllable-timed', and the Germanic languages (German, Dutch, Swedish, etc.) are 'stress-timed', like English.

Each language also has its own set of 'tunes': ways of making the pitch of whole groups of words rise up and dip down. Our brains cleverly fit these tunes round the pattern of stresses. Here is how one English speaker does it. The blobs represent the amount of stress put on each syllable.

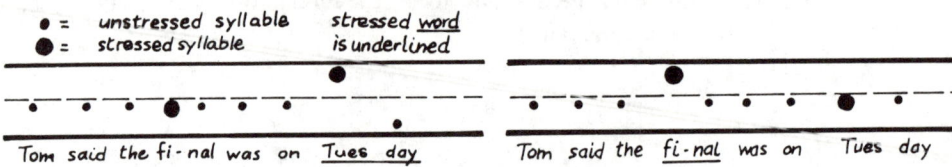

 On the cassette are examples of the six other languages described in this book. In each case the speaker is describing his or her house. Listen for differences in stress or tune. You may be able to decide which three tend to be syllable-timed and which three stress-timed. You may even be able to sort out which language is which.

14

5 Writing the sounds down

Roughly speaking, the letters of the Roman alphabet stand for sounds. English *fat*, Dutch *film* and Spanish *foto* all begin with an *f* sound. But letters and sounds do not always relate one-to-one:

One letter: various sounds
Examples: the *s* sounds in *sorry*, *sure* and *realise*; the *a* sounds in *bad* and *father*.

Different letters: one sound
Examples: the [i:] sound in *tea*, Northern English *Polly* and *feet*; the [sh] sound in *sugar* and *action*.

More than one letter: single sound
Examples: the [f] in *photo*; the [u] in *tooth* and *could*.

P Some sounds cease to be heard as words change their pronunciation. Which letters are no longer sounded in *knight*, *doubt*, *science* and *reign*? This kind of thing happens because individual sounds can change or disappear as a language develops, but it's harder to alter a language's written form – to keep it in step with pronunciation changes. Why should this be? List as many reasons as you can.

Of the languages which developed from Latin, the written forms of Italian and Spanish show their pronunciation reasonably well. So Italian and Spanish children may be faster than English-speaking children at learning to read and write.

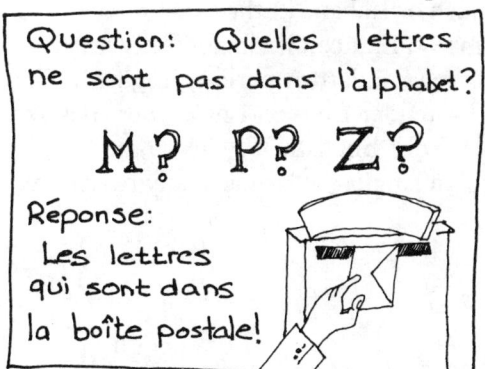

 What about French?
Read this French joke and then listen to it on the cassette. How close is the written form to the spoken form?

15

[S]

[P]

All these different accents just get in the way. People should be made to speak PROPERLY!

What do YOU think?

[G]

[P]

The written forms of Dutch, German and Swedish are quite good at showing pronunciation. Written English is not so helpful. Until the introduction of printing, in the 15th century, English was written much as it was spoken. Since then spoken English has changed enormously, and written English hasn't kept up with these changes. Choose any piece of English that you like. Read it out loud and compare its written and spoken forms. If you were to re-design English spelling, how would you change the piece you have examined? Write a few lines using your newly invented spellings. Show them to your neighbour. Can he or she read them? English spelling can sometimes give you 'eye-messages' where the sounds alone can be confusing:
How long will this rein/reign/rain last?

People living in different parts of a country use different forms of pronunciation. So the *o* sound of the English word *go* will sound different in the mouth of a Scot, a Yorkshire person, or someone brought up in Wales. You can check this by choosing a piece of English and inviting people with different accents (perhaps there are some in your class) to read it out.

Other languages can also be pronounced in a variety of ways. A North German might find it hard to understand the way German is spoken in parts of Southern Germany, or in Switzerland, and the French you hear along the Mediterranean coast sounds different from the French spoken in Paris, not to mention the French you hear in Belgium or the French-speaking parts of Canada.

In your foreign language lessons you learn to speak standard German, French, Spanish or Italian. In the same way, schoolchildren in Germany, France, Spain and Italy learn to speak standard English (or standard American English). They certainly do not learn Eastender London English, or Glasgow English, or Jewish New York English. Why learn the standard form of a foreign language? List as many reasons as you can.

Language family likeness

Whilst concentrating on differences between the six languages, we should not forget their family likeness. Here are some examples of languages outside the European family. Can you name them and say where each is spoken (match them up with the capital cities below)?

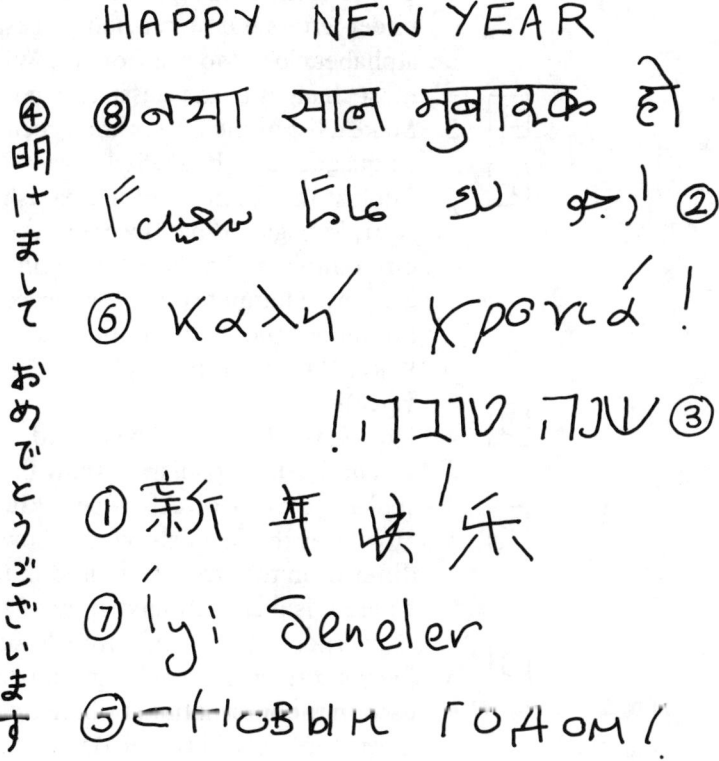

1. Beijing 2. Cairo 3. Tel Aviv 4. Tokyo 5. Moscow
6. Athens 7. Ankara 8. Dehli

G How do all the languages differ from English? Look first at the writing. Do any of the world languages listed above use the Roman alphabet? European languages do. Can you suggest why? (How far did the great Roman Empire extend?)

Now look at the direction in which the writing goes. Which of the languages listed above is NOT written from left to right?

17

Roman writing has been 'improved' in various ways. As you work through Units 6 to 11 try to find the answers to these questions:

[S] 1 'Improving' the Roman alphabet: the Roman alphabet consisted of 23 letters (A B C D E F G H I K L M N O P Q R S T V X Y Z). English has three extra letters. What are they? The Romans made no use of accents or other marks on or under letters. Of our six languages, which one uses an alphabet closest to the Roman? Which of them has made most changes to the classical Roman alphabet?

[S] 2 Make a list of the letters and accents used in the six languages described which were NOT used by the Romans.

[P] 3 Look at the accent used in Spanish (el atlántico, Córdoba, aquí, Málaga). What does the accent show? How is it different from the accents used in French (un élève, un garçon, la tempête). Do these accents tell you how to pronounce the sound of the letter or whether it is STRESSED when spoken (that is, given more weight by the voice)?

[G] 4 Do you think it would be a good idea if English had an accent like the Spanish to show the stressed syllable when spoken (Líverpool, Aberdéen, kílometre, gasómeter)?

[P] 5 How does the Spanish accent showing the stressed syllable differ from the stress sign used in the Oxford Dictionary, where it is placed immediately AFTER the stressed syllable (Liv'erpool, Aberdeen', unfor'tunate)?

[G] 6 Do you prefer the stress sign in front of the syllable as used in the International Phonetic Alphabet (['liverpu:l], [aber'di:n], [ən'fɔ:tjuneit])?

18

6 The Dutch language
De nederlandse taal

Tune into Dutch

goede Dag
mijn naam is Pieter Jans
ik kome uit Rotterdam
mijn hobby is ijsschaatsen

[S] When something sounds difficult or odd we might say 'that's all double Dutch'. It's strange that Dutch has this reputation for being difficult, because it's a close relative of English. Look again at the language map on page 10. Although it can still take years to speak and understand Dutch well, everyday Dutch can be easy to follow. Work out what these questions and answers mean, and match them up correctly.

Hoe laat is het?   Hij is vijftien.
Kan ik U helpen?   Het is middernacht.
Hoe oud is Jan?   Ja, ik kan mijn deur niet openmaken.

BEVER ZWERFSPORT
Specialist in lichtgewicht tenten (Bever, Mentora, Nomad, North Face, Lowe, Fjällräven); 130 rugzakmodellen; donzen en synth. slaapzakken; wind-regen-warmte-kleding; kano's en toebehoren; bergsportmaterialen en berg(wandel)schoenen; kaarten, reisgidsen, etc. etc.
DEN HAAG Calandplein 4, 070-883700
Bever Boek & Kaart 070-885639. Bus 18 v.HS/CS
ROTTERDAM Oudedijk 243, Tram 7 v. C.S.
ARNHEM Utrechtsestr. 5, t.o. station
UTRECHT Biltstraat 96 per 4 feb. 86
        Balijelaan 12 Bus 1,5 v.C.S.
Katalogus op aanvraag

[P] Can you name five things you might be able to buy in the shop advertising here?

Dutch is spoken by fifteen million people living in the Netherlands (also called Holland), and by six million people in the Northern half of Belgium. Belgian Dutch is also called Flemish.

Dutch has links with English, but even stronger links with German. The kind of German spoken in North Germany, near the Netherlands, is very like Dutch:

DUTCH	*pad*	*heet*
NORTH GERMAN	*pad*	*heit*
STANDARD GERMAN	*Pfad*	*heiß*
ENGLISH	*path*	*hot*

The Netherlands and Belgium may not be very powerful countries today, but between about 1600 and 1700 the Dutch-speaking lands were one of the most important powers in the world. The Netherlands' strength came from its huge fleet of sailing ships, which carried cargoes all over the world. It's no wonder that Dutch words to do with ships and sea travel passed into other languages, including English. What words have we got from *jacht, schoener, schipper, dek, dok* and *pomp*?

Here are some definitions, taken from a dictionary, of other words which came into English from Dutch. Which English word is being described in each case?

★★★★★★ Wooden frame to support picture, blackboard, etc. (from Dutch *ezel* = German *Esel*, English *ass*, *donkey* [animals which carry burdens])

★★★★★★ Strong spirit distilled from wine (17th century *brand-wine*, from Dutch *brandewijn* = English 'burnt [distilled] wine')

Dutch people sailed to America, and settled in *Nieuw Amsterdam*, later renamed New York by English settlers. Some words which Dutch gave to American English are:

cookie   boss   snoop   spook
Santa Claus   sleigh   dollar

Dutch people also settled in South Africa, where a form of Dutch known as Afrikaans developed. It is now a separate language spoken by three million white people there. Look at a map of South Africa and find place names which mean 'John's Town', 'Flower Fountain', and 'Welcome'. Can you find the place which the Afrikaners call the 'Kaap de Goeie Hoop'?

The Netherlands and Belgium are small countries, and the total number of Dutch speakers in the world is not very high. So few foreigners see a need to learn Dutch, and many Dutch speakers have learned to speak good English in order to keep in touch with the world outside their own country. But there is a new pride in the Dutch language. The Netherlands and Belgium have together set up the Council for the Dutch Language.

 These advertisements were put out by a Dutch supermarket. For each one list the words and phrases which you understand, putting the English translation next to each item ('2,88' means 'two guilders and eighty-eight cents'.)

 The German language
Die deutsche Sprache

guten Morgen
mein Name ist Heidi Wolf
ich bin zwölf Jahre alt | I am twelve years old
ich komme aus München
ich habe vier Brüder

 German makes use of a special kind of written accent called an Umlaut (ä, ö, ü). Letters with and without an Umlaut are pronounced differently. Listen to *Bruder* (*brother*) and *Brüder* (*brothers*) on the cassette. Also compare *guten* and *München*, *komme* and *zwölf*.

German and Dutch are similar in many ways. Look at these lines from a textbook used to teach Dutch to German students. To help you understand, the literal English 'translation' keeps to the Dutch word order.

Piet de Vries heeft een wekker, Peter de Vries hat einen Wecker,	(Peter de Vries has an alarm-clock)
die hij elke morgen af laat lopen. den er jeden Morgen ablaufen läßt.	(which he each morning off lets go.)
Vanochtend hoort hij hem niet. Heute morgen hört er ihn nicht.	(This morning hears he it not.)
Maar's avonds vraagt hij altijd Aber abends bittet er immer	(But of an evening asks he always)
aan zijn moeder, om in elk geval om zeven uur seine Mutter, auf jeden Fall um sieben Uhr	(his mother in any case at seven o'clock)
aan zijn deur te kloppen. an seine Tür zu klopfen.	(at his door to knock.)
Daardoor komt hij toch op tijd Dadurch kommt er noch rechtzeitig	(That way comes he still on time)
uit zijn bed. aus seinem Bett.	(out of his bed.)

G Where, in the example, is the order of the German words different from the order of the Dutch words? Discuss how you would change the English to make it sound right. How many of the 47 Dutch words in the text seem in some way SIMILAR to their German counterparts, and how many seem COMPLETELY DIFFERENT?

Find the Dutch and German for these words and set them out in pairs:

off   go   evening   seven   knock

What do they show you about '*v*'s and '*f*'s on the one hand and '*b*'s and '*p*'s on the other? What can you say about the '*d*'s and '*t*'s in the Dutch and German for *mother*, *door* and *bed*? Listen to the text on page 22. Are there German words which seem to be pronounced EXACTLY like their Dutch counterparts? What can you say about the way Germans use capital letters?

For every speaker of Dutch there are five speakers of German: about a hundred million altogether. German is the only language, or the main language, of four European countries.

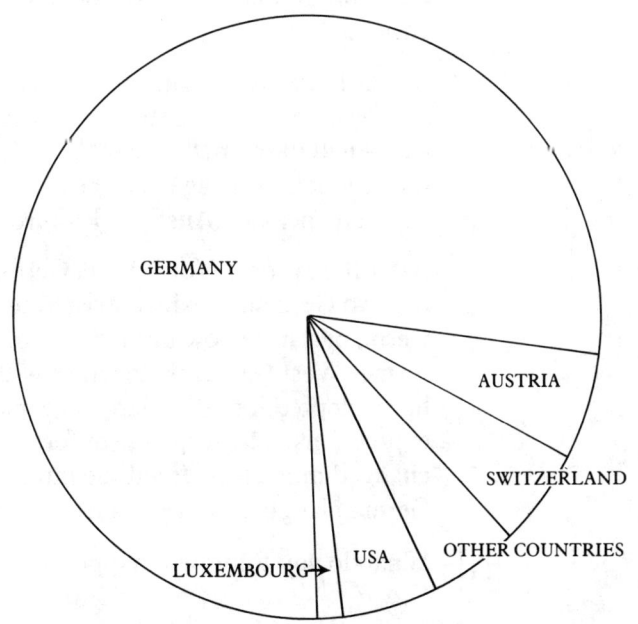

German developed only slowly into a single language understood by all Germans. Until the 17th century there was a patchwork of differing Germanic languages and dialects covering a huge part of Central Europe. There was no one Germany, only a collection of separate kingdoms, dukedoms and cities.

Most of the rulers of these states spoke and wrote French amongst themselves until the 18th century. German, they thought, was too vulgar. At the same time, teachers, scholars and churchmen preferred Latin to German or French.

German was the language of the people and so could not be held back forever. But it could not become the language of power and influence until there was a form of German which everyone agreed on. During the 15th and 16th centuries it was found that one dialect, East Central German, was a good compromise between other forms found in the north and south. It was made more popular by the invention of the printing press in the early 1400s, and by Martin Luther, who translated the Bible into East Central German between 1522 and 1534.

By about 1700 East Central German was known simply as German. Writers, lawyers and churchmen began to use and enrich it.

By 1871 one state, Prussia, had gained control over almost all the German-speaking states in the north. These states became a new nation, named *Deutschland* (Germany): a single country with a single language. To the south was the weaker, mostly German-speaking Austrian Empire.

After the Second World War, Germany became divided into the two Germanies which existed until 1990. These two Germanies have now unified to form one country again. The former West Germans (together with the Austrians and Swiss) have adopted into their language many English and American expressions. The language of former East Germany has changed much less. It will be interesting to see how the German language develops from now on.

|G| What do you think will happen?

[P] Some German words have come directly into English. Here are clues to two of them:
Dachs means *badger*, so what kind of dog used to be sent into their burrows?
Berg means *mountain*. But what kind of 'mountain' floats in Arctic waters?

[S] These words also come from German. Find out what they mean:

hamburger   kaputt   kitsch   schmalz   blitz

German-speaking emigrants began arriving in North America in the 17th century. In Pennsylvania today 250,000 of their descendants speak a dialect known as Pennsylvania Dutch ('Dutch', in this case, means 'Deutsch' – German). This dialect has 'Germanised' many English words and expressions.

STANDARD GERMAN	ENGLISH	PENNSYLVANIA DUTCH
genau	(exactly)	xäctly
beschäftigt	(busy)	büssig
Wieviel Uhr ist es?	(What time is it?)	Was Zeit iss's?
Mir fehlt nichts	(I'm all right)	Ich bin alrecht

[P] Here's a piece of German which is very similar to English. Work out what it means.

 Es ist Neujahrstag. Schiffskapitän Thomas Schneider ist allein auf der Brücke. Aus der Schiffskantine kommt Partymusik. Es ist Vollmond und das Wetter ist klar. Was ist das? Eisberge! Stopp alle Motore! Krach! Eiskaltes Wasser strömt in das Schiff und es beginnt zu sinken. Zwölf Seemänner und eine Katze springen in ein Boot. Ach nein! Das Boot ist zu voll! . . . Dann wacht der Kapitän auf. Er ist im Bett, und das war alles ein Traum.

8 The Swedish language
Svenska språket

hej!
jag heter Ingrid Jespersen
jag bor i Stockholm, | I live in Stockholm,
i Sverige | in Sweden
mina hobbyer är att dansa
och cycla

Swedish, like German, makes use of written accents. The letters å, ä and ö are different from a and o. The Swedish alphabet ends like this: x y z å ä ö. Listen to the sounds which the last three letters represent: Olofs hår är grönt. – Olof's hair is green.

In the north of Europe three North Germanic languages are spoken: Swedish, Danish and Norwegian. In language family terms they are sisters, and cousins of German, Dutch and English.

SWEDISH-SPEAKERS	8 million in Sweden 350,000 in Finland
DANISH-SPEAKERS	5 million in Denmark
NORWEGIAN-SPEAKERS	4 million (two kinds of Norwegian: 1 *Bokmål* (meaning 'book language' or 'literary language') with strong Danish flavour – Norway once under Danish rule 2 *Nynorsk* (formerly 'landsmål', meaning 'country language') – 'new' nationalist form of Norwegian developed deliberately in early 19th century from country dialects)

[S] Look up Norway, Sweden and Denmark (often described together as Scandinavia) in an atlas. Find Iceland and Finland, which are sometimes also thought of as being part of Scandinavia. Icelandic, with 240,000 speakers, is another North Germanic language. Can you spot Iceland? In the world today there are about 18 million speakers of North Germanic languages. Finnish is part of a completely different language family: Finno-Ugrian.

If a Swede, a Dane and a Norwegian were to chat together, each in his or her own language, they would understand one another fairly well. They would use very similar words and word patterns. (Compare the Swedish, Danish and Norwegian words on page 11.) But they would need to listen hard because of pronunciation differences, and there might be a few problems with 'false friends'. *Blöt*, for example, means *wet* in Swedish, but *blød* (Danish) and *bløt* (Norwegian) mean *weak, soft* and in slang they mean *silly*. So Swedes need to watch what they say if they get wet in Norway!

These three languages developed from Norse, the language of the Vikings, who populated Scandinavia between about 750 and 1050.

In the 8th and 9th centuries Vikings arrived in the British Isles, introducing many Norse words to the Anglo-Saxon language already spoken there. Here are some of the 900 or so Norse words which we still use today:

low	ill	wrong	law	husband
fellow	*bag*	*egg*	*cake*	*skill*
skull	*skin*	*skirt*	*scare*	*scold*
scowl	*take*	*give*	*get*	

 Which part of a house gets its name from Norse *vindauga* (*wind-eye*)? Which seafaring words come from the Norse word *skip*? Which word, to do with the plundering ways of the early Vikings, comes from the Norse *rann* (*house*) and *sækja* (*to search*)?

27

[P] Many British place names come from Norse. Find on a map place names ending in -*by* (village), -*thorpe* (outlying farmstead), -*toft* (plot of land), -*thwaite* (woodland clearing) and -*fell* (mountain).

When the age of restless Viking tribes was over, the nations of Sweden, Denmark and Norway gradually emerged. (Until this century Norway was nearly always in the power of one of the other two.) From the 12th century onwards the peoples of Scandinavia came into contact with the powerful traders of Northern Germany, and took in many German words and phrases. In the 18th century came French words, and since then English has been the main language lender.

[P] Thousands of everyday Swedish words can be understood by English speakers. Guess what the words in each of these sets have in common, and what each word means individually.

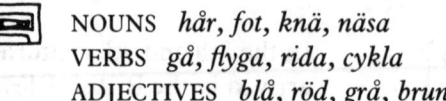

NOUNS   *hår, fot, knä, näsa*
VERBS   *gå, flyga, rida, cykla*
ADJECTIVES   *blå, röd, grå, brun*

On the other hand, Swedish has inherited words from Norse which have no clear links with Dutch, German or English. We can, for example, guess that Dutch *wassen* and German *waschen* mean *to wash*. But the Swedish word is *tvätta*!

Here's a Swedish joke. Two astronauts can't decide where to head for. A little help first: *månen* means *the moon*, and *solen* means *the sun*. The *the* is signified by the *-en* ending.

(*Två astronauter, Ingrid och Olof,
sitter i ett rymdskepp* (= *space ship*).)
'Vi flyger till månen', säger Ingrid.
'Nej, vi flyger till solen', säger Olof.
'Vad? Solen är för varm. Den skulle
bränna upp oss!'
'Nej', säger Olof, 'Jag är inte dum!
Vi flyger vid (*at*) midnatt!'

28

Sweden is now a country of many languages. Schoolchildren in Sweden have the right to be taught their mother tongue or home language from the age of five. So, the children of Finnish immigrant workers are taught Finnish; those of political refugees from Latin America (of which there are quite a number) are taught Spanish. In certain cases, where there are a large number of, say, Finnish speakers in the same school, nearly all the subjects are taught in the home language. And of course, all Swedish children learn English at school; they are also used to seeing films and television in English and to hearing it on the radio and sung by pop bands.

9 The Italian language

La lingua italiana

buon giorno!	
mi chiamo Giovanna Bartolini	
come stai?	how are you?
sto bene, grazie	I'm fine, thanks
arrivederci	goodbye

For English-speakers Italian is one of the easiest languages to learn. Many Italian word patterns are like ours, Italian spelling is regular, and it's quite a reliable guide to pronunciation.

You have seen how everyday German, Dutch or Swedish words can be very like English words. But Italian is a Romance language, and many everyday Italian words are unlike anything in English. What, for example, do you make of this Italian proverb?

Una rondine non fa primavera.
The same proverb in German is much more like English:
Eine Schwalbe macht noch keinen Sommer.
One swallow doesn't make a summer.
(The Italian word *rondine* does mean *swallow*, but *primavera* means, not *summer*, but *spring!*)

29

The majority of words in Italian have a Latin origin. In English about half of the words have a Latin (or Greek) origin. So many Italian words look familiar to us.

 Read the following piece of Italian and list all the Italian words that are like English words.

 L'Italia è una nazione di cinquantacinque (55) milioni di abitanti. È una repubblica con una costituzione democratica. Le regioni industriali sono nel nord. Le regioni agricole, relativamente povere, sono nel sud.

The Italian words in your list are similar to many French words. English contains words of French origin (brought in by the Normans). So sometimes we can understand Italian words through the French words in our language.

NORMAN FRENCH   *feste*
MIDDLE FRENCH   *feast*
ITALIAN   *festa*

The *s* disappeared from the French word at the end of the 12th century (MODERN FRENCH: *fête*).

We can also understand Italian through the Latin words that came into English; long after Latin had died out as anyone's mother tongue, it was still used by educated people all over Europe. Some of their Latin words passed into English in this way.

Italian developed from the kind of Latin we call Vulgar Latin. There were two different kinds of Latin:

CLASSICAL LATIN	VULGAR LATIN
was spoken and written	was spoken but hardly ever written
was rather elegant, even 'posh', and had complicated inflection rules	had fewer rules, more word-adding, and varied from place to place
was the language of educated people	was the language of millions of ordinary people
was spoken in Rome and certain parts of the Roman Empire, notably North Africa	was spoken all over the Roman Empire

By about the sixth century Classical Latin had died out as a spoken language, and it was from Vulgar Latin that Italian, and the other Romance languages shown on page 11, developed.

The two kinds of Latin often had very different words for the same thing. *Horse* in Classical Latin was *equus*, from which English has the rather grand words *equine* and *equestrian*. But it was the Vulgar Latin word for a horse, *caballus*, which passed into Italian, becoming *cavallo*. It became *cheval* in French.

|G| Which English words, to do with horses, have come from *cavallo* and *cheval*?

Here's another example:

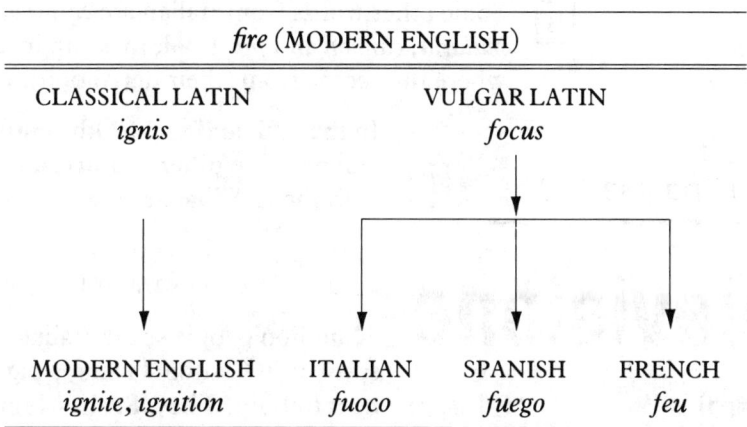

When The Roman Empire broke up, spoken, everyday ('vulgar') Latin developed into different regional dialects. For example a citizen from Venice, in the North, could not easily understand someone from Sicily in the South. About 130 years ago, however, the people of the different Italian states began to revolt against their kings and princes, and to form a united democratic Italy. Obviously, in forming a nation a common language is of great help. The dialect spoken in the

31

Tuscany region of central Italy was chosen to be the official language, and it was taught throughout the new national school system. This did not go down well with the speakers of other dialects.

About 500 years ago, in Italian city states such as Florence (in Tuscany) and Venice, there was a great flowering of new and exciting ideas in art, technology, architecture, music and poetry. Along with other Europeans, English people became fascinated by this RENAISSANCE, and started using certain Italian words in their own language. Even today, musicians all over the world read their instructions in Italian. They know that *crescendo* means 'growing louder', and that *volti subito* means 'turn the page quickly'. Get hold of a full list of Italian musical terms. What are these Italian words?

G

If you sing by yourself you are singing _ _ _ _ .
A group of three singers is a _ _ _ _ .
Italian for *small* – also the name of a small musical instrument: p _ _ _ _ _ _ .

S

Some other words from Italian are *carnival, umbrella, alarm, malaria, cannon* and *flu*. Look these up in a dictionary and see where they come from (their derivation).

Grazia/pagina 160   P

In the 19th and early 20th centuries many Italians emigrated to other countries, bringing their foods with them. What are these food words?

spa _ _ _ _ _ i   p _ zz _   m _ _ _ r _ _ i
l _ s _ _ _ e   cann _ ll _ _ _   p _ _ ta

televisione

venerdì   12/luglio

Raiuno
13.00 Voglia di musica
13.30 Telegiornale
13.45 Il crollo di Roma – Film
16.30 Il grande teatro del West
17.05 Love story – Telefilm
18.40 Linea verde speciale
20.00 Telegiornale
20.30 Laurel & Hardy: due teste senza cervello

54 million people speak Italian in Italy, and 250,000 speak it in Canton Ticino, a part of Switzerland next to Italy. The USA has 4 million Italian speakers, living in 'Little Italies' in the biggest cities. Australia and Canada have 500,000 Italian speakers each. Britain also has Italian communities, in London, Bedford and Bradford, for example.

Listen to this being read out on the cassette.

10 The Spanish language
La lengua española

buenos días!	hello!
me llamo Carmen González	my name is Carmen González
¿habla usted español?	do you speak Spanish?
soy de Barcelona	I'm from Barcelona
– una ciudad en el norte	– a city in the north

If a word ends in a consonant the last syllable is usually stressed (ciu**dad**, espa**ñol**). If it ends with a vowel (or an *s* or *n*) the second to last syllable is stressed (Barce**lo**na, **nor**te). If a word needs to be stressed in a place you might not expect, an accent lets you know: fan**tás**tico, A**mé**rica.

Spanish is the main language of nineteen countries, with about 290 million speakers. Only Chinese (Mandarin 700 million) and English (300 million) have more. Spain has 33 million Spanish speakers, but South and Central America have 264 million Spanish speakers.

Spanish and Italian are Romance languages, and are similar in many ways:

SPANISH
América del Sur es un continente de contrastes,
de cosas fantásticas y maravillosas.
ITALIAN
Il Sud America e un continente di contrasti,
di cose fantastice e meravigliose.

In some ways Spanish became more different from Latin than Italian did and certain sound change rules were established. For example, Latin *f* became Spanish *h*. Latin *filius* (*son*) changed to *figlio* in Italian, but to *hijo* in Spanish. Following the same pattern, Latin *folia* (*leaf*) became Spanish *hoja*, and Latin *fundus* (*deep*) became Spanish *hondo*.

Arabs from Africa invaded Spain in 711 and controlled the country for nearly 700 years. About 4000 Arab words passed into Spanish, but few word patterns did. Most Spanish words from Arabic begin with a tell-tale *a* or *al*, which is the Arabic for *the*. A few Arabic words have also passed into English (but not always by way of Spanish).

Ar: al-koh'l
Sp: alcohol

Ar: alqualiy
Sp: álcali

ARABIC	SPANISH	ENGLISH
al-quton	algodón	cotton
al-sukkar	azucar	sugar
al-jabr	algebra	algebra

Chemists (once called alchemists) use alcohol and alkalis.

[G] The Arabs in Spain were part of a great and knowledgeable empire. They gave us their number system. How is the Arabic system (for example, 8, 9, 10, 11) better than the Roman one (VIII, IX, X, XI)? They also gave Spanish words to do with their Muslim religion and these have become quite commonplace in everyday Spanish. Even today, a Christian Spaniard who wants something badly may say '¡Ojalá que . . . !', perhaps not realising that it means 'Allah let it happen that . . . !'.

[S] The Arabs were finally driven out of Spain in 1492. Shortly after this, in the 16th century, Spanish and Portuguese adventurers found rich new lands in Central and South America. They believed that there was some marvellous 'Kingdom of Gold' to be discovered. Here is a passage about Spanish explorers of that time. Match up the words in italics with the Spanish words in the margin.

34

cargas
galeones
patatas
conquistadores
maíz
chocolate
El Dorado
cacao

The *Spanish conquerors* of the Americas never found the legendary *Kingdom of Gold*, but they did send home *large ships* with *cargoes* of gold and silver, along with new foods. There was a *new kind of corn*, and a *new root vegetable*. There was a *dark substance made from powdered seeds*, and which could be made into *something sweet to eat*.

Look at a map which names the countries of Central and South America. Find Spanish-speaking countries whose names mean:
(a) The Rich Coast
(b) The Saviour (meaning Christ)
(c) Made of Silver (from the Spanish word *argentino*)
(d) The Equator (the imaginary line which makes a great circle round the earth)
(e) Land of Christopher Columbus

Although most of the countries in Central and South America are Spanish-speaking, the biggest and fastest-growing country in South America is Brazil, and its main language is Portuguese.

The Spanish-speaking areas stretch up through Mexico and well into the United States. 60% of all Californians speak Spanish as their mother tongue. Find out about the original meanings of these American place names:

San Francisco   Florida   Los Angeles   Nevada   El Paso

These Spanish words passed into American English. What do they mean?

gringo   rodeo   estampida   cañón
lazo   corral   amigo   bronco

The Spanish of the different South American countries is spoken with a variety of accents and has produced words which are different from the Spanish of Spain. When the letter *c* comes before an *e* or an *i* most Spaniards make it sound like a *th*. But South Americans pronounce that *c* as an *s*. Try pronouncing the word *información* first as a Spaniard would, then as a South American would. The *th* heard in Spain is called the *ceceo*, which means *lisp*. The South American *s* sound for *c* is called the *seseo*.

35

DOMINGO, 30
1ª Cadena

9,30 **Concierto**.
10,30 **Santa Misa** y Bendición Urbi et Orbi, desde la Basílica de San Pedro de Roma.
12,30 **Estudio estadio**. Incluye hockey sobre patines (encuentro internacional), motociclismo (Campeonato de España), golf (Campeonato de España, APG).
15,00 **Telediario**.

LUNES, 31
1ª Cadena

10,00 **Directo en la noche**. (Repetición).
11,30 **Dinastía**. (59). Blake denuncia a Alexis que se han manejado cifras fraudulentas en la fusión de las dos compañías. Steven va a visitar a Claudia al sanatorio. Alexis ofrece dinero a Mark para que abandone a Fallon, pero el se niega. Krystle quiere asentar las cosas entre Blake y su hijo Steven y prepara una cena familiar.
12,25 **Avance telediario**.
12,30 **Teletexto**.
13,30 **Programación regional**.

 Here is part of the television section in a Spanish magazine from Spain. You can hear it read out on the cassette. See how much you can understand with no help. Then you'll hear the programmes explained in detail on the cassette. How well did you do?

 This is a school timetable for 13- to 14-year-old Spanish children. Work out which subject is which. How does it compare with your own school timetable?

	lunes	martes	miércoles	jueves	viernes
9.00–10.00	matemática	lenguaje	matemática	lenguaje	matemática
10.00–11.00	lenguaje	matemática	lenguaje	matemática	lenguaje
11.00–11.30	RECREO				
11.30–12.30	formación religiosa	idioma extranjero (inglés)	ciencias naturales	idioma extranjero (inglés)	ciencias sociales
15.00–16.00	educación física y deportes	formación religiosa	idioma extranjero (inglés)	½h ciencias sociales ½h ciencias naturales	educación física y deportes
16.00–16.20	RECREO				
16.20–17.20	ciencias sociales	expresión plástica (dibujo)	educación física y deportes	expresión plástica (dibujo)	ciencias naturales

36

11 The French language
La langue française

Tune into French

bonjour!	hello!
je m'appelle Martin Duval	I'm called Martin Duval
j'habite Tours, en France	I live in Tours, in France
j'ai un frère, Jacques	I have one brother, Jacques
j'ai deux soeurs, Hélène et Françoise	I have two sisters, Hélène and Françoise
Françoise travaille à l'hôpital	Françoise works at the hospital

Now meet Astérix, the famous French cartoon hero. This is what he might have said:

Je m'appelle Astérix. Aidé par une potion magique du Druide Panoramix, je défends mon village contre l'ennemi romain. Quel passetemps agréable!

Astérix fights off the Romans. But he couldn't fight off the Romans' language: he speaks in French, which developed from the Romans' language: Vulgar Latin.

In the fifth century the Romans abandoned the area which is now France, and Germanic tribes moved in. The most powerful were the Franks, who gave France its name. In the late eighth century Charlemagne, King of the Franks, built up a new empire. It was Christian, and its main language was a dialect of French. Charlemagne's empire fell apart but French survived as an important language.

In 1066 French-speaking Normans invaded Anglo-Saxon-speaking England, and stayed. The two languages did not mix easily. The Normans were the masters, and Anglo-Saxons learned Norman French if they wanted to get on. For 300 years Norman French was the language of the manor houses, the schools, the law courts, and of Parliament and the king. Anglo-Saxon was still widely spoken, but rarely written down.

The two languages eventually came together. By the 14th century everyone was using Anglo-Saxon words and word patterns, but with Norman French words mixed in. Sometimes a Norman French word blotted out an Anglo-Saxon word. *Eorþcræft* (earth-craft) gave way to *géométrie*, and *Iæcecræft* gave way to *médecine*. Without the Normans we would probably now say *bookskill* instead of *literature*. What do we say instead of *starskill* and *numberskill*?

More often, the new French word settled in alongside an old Anglo-Saxon word, the one having a slightly different meaning from the other. Look at these pairs and try to spot differences in meaning. You might, for example, say that your school is wonderful, but would you say it's miraculous?

words from ANGLO-SAXON	words from FRENCH	modern FRENCH
house	mansion	maison
room	chamber	chambre
folk	people	peuple
start	commence	commencer
teach	instruct	instruire
loving	affectionate	affectionné
wonderful	miraculous	miraculeux (-euse)
go down	descend	descendre

The Anglo-Saxon words which survived the Conquest were mostly basic 'bread and butter' ones. Norman French words were more learned and longer (look at the list above). Which of these do you think is from Anglo-Saxon, and which from French?

smell   perfume   fragrance   stench   stink   odour   aroma

The Norman overlords had costly instruments to measure time precisely so they had words for the smaller divisions of time. On the other hand, the Anglo-Saxon speakers, out in the fields and farmsteads, measured time more roughly.

P Which of these words do you think is from Anglo-Saxon, and which from Norman French?

day   minute   second   night   hour   month

> English land!
> Withdraw!
> This means war!
> Death!

> Norman territory!
> Retreat!
> This signifies conflict!
> Mortality!

Look again at the moon/lune word table on page 12. We can understand many other words (and word patterns) from both the Germanic and Romance language groups – precisely because English is a mixture of Germanic Anglo-Saxon and Norman French. It has given English a doubly rich stock of words.

Even before the 17th century, French was the leading language in Europe, and many learned it as a second language. By the 17th century it had replaced Latin as the major European language of culture and diplomacy. It became a 'world language', used at international meetings, and in quite a few royal households. One German king, Frederick the Great of Prussia (1712–86), wrote poems in French (not very good ones) and kept showing them to the French writer Voltaire. Voltaire once wrote that, at Frederick's court, 'l'allemand est pour les soldats et pour les chevaux' – 'German is for the soldiers and horses'.

French has now been overtaken by English as the most widely spoken 'world language'. But French is still the native language of 75 million people round the world. 51 million speak it in France, 6 million in Canada, 4 million in Belgium, 1.3 million in Switzerland and 1 million in the USA.

S French is an official language in many countries once ruled by France, although not everyone in these countries speaks it, and it often has to be learned as a second language. Look at a map of Africa. If you know French you can talk to people in twenty or so African countries. These include Morocco, Algeria and Tunisia in the north, and a broad band of countries stretching from Senegal in the west to Zaïre in Central Africa. (French was taken to Zaïre by the Belgians.) A third of all Canadians, mostly in Quebec, speak French as their mother tongue. Find Quebec in your atlas. Which of its cities has a French name meaning 'royal mountain'? Most French-speakers in the USA live in the state of Louisiana. Which of its cities is named after a town in France?

12 How do languages compare?

Tune into the grammar

In science classes we find it interesting to investigate the 'rules' of physics or chemistry. In a similar way grammar investigates 'rules' or patterns in the things people say and write which help to show how our language works, and how English compares with other languages.

You may say: 'But we do interesting experiments in science. How can we do experiments with grammar!?' Try this one. It will prove that we all operate, every day, a complicated grammar 'rule' in English that we did not even know existed.

Order of words

An experiment: Work in groups of equal numbers. Here are two mixed-up lists of words.

put   he   on   jacket   green   trendy   new   tweed   his
put   she   on   blouse   blue   cosy   old   nylon   her

In your group take the mixed-up lists of words and write them out to form two sentences, putting the words in the order that the majority of the group feels is the most natural. Compare your results with those of the other groups. We can predict that all the groups will make exactly the same two sentences from the two mixed-up lists. (To see what these are, look at the bottom of the page.)

spot the pattern

You will see that each sentence has a NOUN (something to wear) and a number of words telling more about the noun (*his/her*; *green/blue*; *trendy/cosy* etc.) Can you find them?

The grammatical name for these describing words is ADJECTIVE. And a useful way to refer to a phrase made up of NOUN + ADJECTIVE is NOUN PHRASE (or NP for short).

He put on his trendy new green tweed jacket.
She put on her cosy old blue nylon blouse.

40

[G] Discuss in groups any similarities you can find between the two NPs you have made. For instance, is there a pattern in the order of the words? (For example, where do the colour adjectives fit in the two lists?)

You have all agreed on the order of the adjectives in two sentences you have never seen before. How could this be explained?

More on word order

Take another look at units 9, 10 and 11 (the ROMANCE languages) and see if you can spot examples of NPs similar to these:

the white house	FRENCH	la maison blanche
	SPANISH	la casa blanca
	ITALIAN	la casa bianca

the white wine	FRENCH	le vin blanc
	SPANISH	el vino blanco
	ITALIAN	il vino bianco

[G] In these NPs you will spot an obvious difference between English and the other languages. Does the colour adjective come before or after the noun? (In Units 6 to 8 on the GERMANIC languages, Swedish, Dutch and German, you may be able to find NPs in which the order of NOUN + ADJECTIVE is more like English. Discuss in your groups and see if you can suggest why this is so.)

Grammatical gender

Word order is not the only point to notice about *la maison blanche / le vin blanc* etc. There are two other ways in which these NPs are different from English.

Where English has '**the** house' / '**the** wine', French has two different words: **le** and **la**. You probably know that this is because ALL nouns in French (as in Italian and Spanish) belong to either the MASCULINE or FEMININE gender (GENDER here simply means something like 'kind' of noun); **le** and **la** are markers which show the 'kind' or gender to which each noun belongs. There are also two genders in Dutch and Swedish which are called COMMON and NEUTER.

	COMMON	NEUTER
SWEDISH	solen (the sun)	mån (the moon)
DUTCH	de zon (the sun)	het maan (the moon)

German is the one language of our six which is like Latin in having THREE genders:

	MASCULINE	FEMININE	NEUTER
GERMAN	der Mond (the moon)	die Sonne (the sun)	das Licht (the light)
LATIN	sol (the sun)	luna (the moon)	lumen (the light)

In French, Spanish and Italian *the moon* is feminine (*la lune* / *la luna* / *la luna*) and *the sun* is masculine (*le soleil* / *el sol* / *il sole*), just the opposite of the genders in German. What do you think this shows us about grammatical gender?

In all this English is the 'odd man out'; grammatical gender does not exist. It is true that human beings and animals in English are 'male' or 'female', that is belong to different 'sexes'. This use of *he/she* is sometimes extended to things we are fond of. What are ships called at the launching ceremony? But this is not quite the same as the gender to which ALL nouns belong in the other European languages.

In my German dictionary it says that the gender of 'girl' is neuter (das Mädchen) Must be a mistake! Girls are feminine!

Is he right?!

[G] You have to write a grammar book for children aged 8. Explain the difference between male/female and grammatical gender.

[G] We said above that English is the 'odd man out' in Europe – the ONLY language whose nouns do not show grammatical gender. How does this affect foreign learners beginning to speak English. How is their job different from your job when you begin to learn, say, French?

'Agreement' within the NP

Look again at these phrases:

| the white house | **la** maison blanche | **la** casa blanca |
| the white wine | **le** vin blanc | **el** vino blanco |

You will notice that the adjective *white* in English is spelt in the same way with *house* as with *wine*. Its spelling (and the way we say it) never changes. And in the other languages? There is 'agreement' between noun and adjective. Look at some more examples showing how adjectives 'agree' with the noun in the NP:

ma jolie petite robe blanche
mon joli petit soulier blanc

Find the noun in each of these NPs (French words for *dress/shoe*). Which adjectives tell:

it is *mine* / it is *pretty* / it is *white*?

Notice that *blanche/blanc* (adjectives of colour) come AFTER the noun; commonly used adjectives, like *joli/jolie*, come BEFORE the noun as in English. But whatever their position, ALL adjectives 'agree' in gender with the noun. It is the same in Spanish:

nuestra querida pequeña casa blanca (our dear little white house)
nuestro querido pequeño perro blanco (our dear little white dog)

But the adjectives in the NP can 'agree' with the noun in another way, too. Look at some more examples.

Singular and plural

FRENCH les robes blanches sont excellentes
        les vins blancs sont excellents

SPANISH las vestidas blancas son magníficas
        los vinos blancos son magníficos

Look at the '*s*' on *les robes / les vins*. What does it mean? It means that there is more than one dress, more than one wine. In grammatical terms, when an '*s*' is added, a SINGULAR noun

43

ENG.	goose ~~X~~ *geese*
DU.	gan~~z~~en
GER.	Gä"nse
SW.	g~~ä~~ gäss
IT.	oc~~X~~ oche
SP.	ganso s
FR.	oies

becomes PLURAL. Now look at the adjectives. There are two things to notice. What are they? In English, do adjectives ever have either a feminine or a plural form?

Of course, the noun in English has a plural form and this is usually shown by adding an 's'. But is this the only way? What about the plural of *the mouse, the goose, the child*?

In Units 6 to 11 you will find that other languages have a number of different ways of marking the plural of nouns.

FRENCH	le cheval (the horse) – can you find the plural (see page 39)
SWEDISH	en flicka / tre flickor (a girl / three girls) ett glas / tre glas (a glass / three glasses) ett bi / tre bin (a bee / three bees)
GERMAN	der Mann / die Männer (the man / the men)

Look again at Units 6 and 9 and find how plurals of nouns are marked in Dutch and Italian.

Spanish is the ONLY European language which ALWAYS marks the plural of nouns (and adjectives) with 's'. Are there other ways in which Spanish seems a more 'regular' language than the others?

When gender shows the meaning of a noun

In some languages two words may be spelt the same but mean different things. The gender often marks the difference. In French, *le livre* means *the book*; *la livre* means *the pound*.

How do we know what a sentence means?

Look at these sentences:

the dog bites the man
the man bites the dog

How do you know who did the biting (the doer or the SUBJECT) and who was bitten (the one who was 'done to' or the OBJECT)?

In many other languages the order of words works just as in English:

FRENCH   le chien mord le chat
         le chat mord le chien

Now look at these sentences in Latin:

servum laudat dominus
laudat servum dominus
dominus servum laudat

dominus = master
Meister = master

These all mean the same: 'The master praises the servant.' How do we know that? Obviously the order of the words has nothing to do with it in this case.

German is like Latin in marking with a different ending the JOB that words do in the sentence. (The grammatical name for these jobs is CASE.) While Latin distinguishes six different cases (and so six different possible endings for any noun), German has four. They are shown in this table.

Let's get rid of case endings and word order. Then fun some really have we could!

CASE	JOB DONE	LATIN	GERMAN
nominative	subject of verb	domin**us**	**der** Meister
vocative	person spoken to	domin**e**	
accusative	object of verb	domin**um**	**den** Meister
genitive	means 'of' the noun	domin**i**	**des** Meisters
dative	means 'to' or 'for' the noun	domin**o**	**dem** Meister
ablative	means 'by', 'with', 'from' the noun	domin**o**	

It is possible, in German, as in Latin, to change the word order without changing the basic meaning of the sentence:

der Hund beißt **den** Mann   the dog bites the man
den Mann beißt **der** Hund   (it is) the man (that) the dog bites

45

It is not the order of words that shows who did the biting but the case markers (**der** showing the subject and **den** showing the object.)

der Mann beißt **den** Hund
the man bites the dog

den Hund beißt **der** Mann
(it is) the dog (that) the man bites

In English the only trace of these nominative and accusative cases showing subject and object is found in the PERSONAL PRONOUNS. These are short words standing for persons or things (e.g. **I** like **him** / **he** likes **me** / **they** like **us** / **we** like **them** / **you** like **him** or **her** or **it** / **she** likes **them** and **us** etc).

|G| In your groups, do this experiment to show you that you know more grammar than you thought you did. Here is a list of SUBJECT PRONOUNS in English. First find the OBJECT PRONOUN corresponding to each one. The first one is done for you. Then make up sentences using each of the object pronouns.

Subject	Object	Example
I	ME	he beats ME
YOU	?	?
HE	?	?
SHE	?	?
IT	?	?
WE	?	?
YOU	?	?
THEY	?	?

If we call the subject of the sentence S, the object O and the verb V, we can show the order of words in this way:

```
  S    V      O
the dog bites the cat
```

[S] Now write out these sentences in the same way (the first one is done for you).

a   dominus servum laudat   S O V
b   servum laudat dominus
c   le professeur aime le chocolat (*aime* means *likes*)
d   der Hund beißt den Mann
e   den Mann beißt der Hund
f   te quiero (*quiero* means *I love*)
g   me quieres (*quieres* means *you love*)
h   has he a book?
i   il a un livre
j   il les aime (he likes them)

Investigating verbs

a Showing who or what

The main word in each sentence is its VERB. We can't have a sentence without one. So it is worthwhile taking a brief look at how verbs behave. We saw in the previous section that in Spanish *quiero* means *I love* and *quieres* means *you love*. What do you notice about the verb ending? Compare the French *je t'aime* and *tu m'aimes* (*I love you* and *you love me*.) This kind of change happens in all European languages, including English! Look at this table.

LATIN	FRENCH	SPANISH	ITALIAN	GERMAN	DUTCH	SWEDISH	ENGLISH
amo	j'aime	quiero	amo	ich liebe	ik houd van	jag elskar	I love
amat	il aime	quiere	ama	er liebt	hij houdt van	han elskar	he loves
amamus	nous aimons	queremos	amamo	wir lieben	wij houden van	vi elskar	we love
amant	ils aiment	quieren	aman	sie lieben	zij houden van	de elskar	they love

[P] Which of the languages above shows fewest changes in its verb endings?
What changes to the ending of the verb does English show?

In three of the languages listed, the verb stands by itself without any subject pronoun to show WHO is loving. Which three languages are they?

The subject pronoun IS sometimes found with the verb in Spanish and Italian but is not necessary.

47

b Showing when – an introduction to TENSE

Look at these examples in Italian:

spingono   they push
spingeranno   they will push
spingevanno   they used to push

Here is the same verb in French:

ils poussent   they push
ils pousseront   they will push
ils poussaient   they used to push

[G] Discuss the differences between the way that English tells when an action takes place and how it is shown in French and Italian. The tense of the verb in *they push* is called the present tense because the action is happening NOW. Can you suggest the names of the tenses for the following:

they are pushing   they used to push
they will push   they pushed
they were pushing

More about nouns

An interesting difference between the Germanic languages (Units 6 to 8 in this book) and the Romance languages (Units 9 to 11) is in the way that words are joined together to make nouns. Compare this list:

ENGLISH	toothbrush	ENGLISH	sunrise	(Germanic)
GERMAN	Zahnbürste	DUTCH	zonsopgang	(Germanic)
FRENCH	brosse à dents	ITALIAN	levar del sole	(Romance)

[G] Discuss these examples in your groups and try to describe in the fewest words the difference between the Germanic and the Romance way of joining words. Look especially at the order of the ideas: *teeth/brushing* and *sun/rising*. Which is placed first in German/Dutch/English? And in French/Italian?

Here is what one German dictionary lists under *snow*.

Schnee[ˈʃneː]*m* snow; (*Ei*~) beaten egg-white; ~**ball** *m* snowball; ~**flocke** *f* snowflake; ~**gestöber** *nt* snowstorm; ~**glöckchen** *nt* snowdrop; ~**kette** *f* (*AUT*) (snow) chain; ~**pflug** *m* snowplough; ~**schmelze** *f* thaw; ~**webe** *f* snowdrift; ~**wittchen** *nt* Snow White.

[G] There are lots more compound words made from *Schnee*.
How would a *Schneeschaufel* help you to clear snow away?
Would you go skiing when it is *schneefrei* or *schneereich*?
What abominable creature is the *Schneemensch*?
And how would a *Schneeschlager* help you to make a cake
(*schlagen* means *to beat*)?

Now compare the above German compound nouns with their names in French:

neige [nɛʒ] *f* snow; **blanc** *m* **de** ~ beaten egg-white; **boule** *f* **de** ~ snowball; **flocon** *m* **de** ~ snowflake; **tempête** *f* **de** ~ snowstorm; **perce-**~ *f* snowdrop; **chaîne** *f* **à** ~ snowchain; **chasse-**~ *m* snowplough; **fonte** *f* **des** ~**s** thaw; **amoncellement** *m* **de** ~ snowdrift; **Blanc de N**~ Snow White.

A snowman in French is *un bonhomme de neige* but *The Abominable Snowman* (of the Himalayan mountains) is *l'abominable homme des neiges*.

[G] Discuss in your groups these two dictionary entries of words connected with snow. Can you see a pattern in the way the German compound words are made? How would you describe the pattern and how does it differ from the French way of making compounds? Which is closest to the English pattern?

Translating meanings

When an English speaker meets the word *snow*, the picture that the word brings to mind will be a picture made up of all the occasions when he or she has seen snow.

[G] Do you think a German speaker meeting the German word *Schnee* will have exactly the same picture of snow in mind? It may be similar but probably not exactly the same. What reasons can you think of that might make the two speakers have different mental pictures (or 'meanings' of the word)?

When a French speaker meets the word *pain* (*loaf of bread*) what picture will it bring to mind? How will it differ from the picture that the word *loaf* brings to your mind, as an English speaker? So does the meaning that a word has for us depend on our experience of meeting or using the thing?

G Discuss this in your groups and try to think of words in English and in other languages which may seem to refer to the same thing but really bring different pictures to mind (for example the dictionary gives *breakfast* in French as *petit déjeuner*; do the two words mean exactly the same kind of meal?)

G If the meaning a word has for us depends on our experience, will some words change their meaning for us as we learn more and get more experience? Can you think of such words? (Clue: think of words like *motherhood* or *fatherhood*; will their meaning change for you as you get first-hand experience?) So does this mean that we continue developing our own understanding of our own language throughout our lives?

Another pitfall is that a word in one language may have several meanings which cannot all be translated by the same word in another language. For example, *down* can mean the *feathers* on a duck, as in *eiderdown*. But in the sentence *he fell down*, *down* tells us how he fell, i.e. it tells us more about the verb, and is called an ADVERB. The French for *down* (*feathers*) is *le duvet*. But beware of writing *il tomba duvet* for *he fell down*! The mistake is easy to make if you trust to a small dictionary which does not give all the meanings. Here is another example of how one word may have several meanings which need different translations:

ENGLISH			FRENCH
road	1	main road between towns	*la route*
	2	road in a town or village	*la rue*
	3	roadway (not pavement)	*la chaussée*
	4	the way to somewhere	*le chemin*
	5	carriageway	*la voie*

P Try making up English sentences showing as many different meanings as you can find for:

common   record   note   glasses   to get on

50

FALSE FRIENDS

Sometimes the translator meets another hazard. One language offers a word which LOOKS very like a word in another language but means something quite different. These have been called 'false friends' (*faux amis*). In Spanish a school subject is *una materia*, not *un sujeto* which looks so tempting (*un sujeto* means a grammatical subject in a sentence; or a person who is being treated by the doctor; or an individual who is *subject* to a government). What does a German really mean when he says in English 'I am becoming a hamster'?

bekommen = to get, receive

The French firm SUPERPLASTIQUE makes plastic model kits for export. Their computer could only translate the instructions word for word. Can you put the translation into good English?

Votre maquette a été sévèrement contrôlée. En cas d'erreur veuillez remplir le bon en lettres capitales et l'adresser à SUPERPLASTIQUE accompagné de coupons réponses internationaux d'un montant de l'affranchissement de trois lettres au tarif en vigueur.

Your model kit has been severely controlled. In case of error please fill up the coupon in letters capitals and address it to SUPERPLASTIQUE accompanied of coupons replies international of an amount of the stamping of three letters at the tariff in vigour.

contrôlé = checked
affranchissement = postage
en vigueur = current

> This is MT2. His mind's a complete blank. But I'm going to type in all the words from my French vocabulary book. Then he'll talk French perfectly. Just like me. Let's start. La tête – head, le nez – nose

Put him right!

13 How English links up

Superbrain isn't just a know-all! He's also a valiant hero! Or is he?!
Superbrain is a made-up word. *Super* comes from Latin, and means *over*, *above* or *extra*. In Italian it is *sopra*. What kind of voice does a soprano have?
In Spanish it is *sobre*. After an earthquake you rescue *sobrevivientes*. What are they? In French *super* has become *sur*. What would your car be if it was *surchauffée*?

WALL came to us with the help of Roman soldiers. It developed from their Latin word *vallum*: a rampart, a wall built to keep the enemy out. But what about the other languages?

DUTCH	muur
GERMAN	Mauer
SWEDISH	mur
ITALIAN	muro
SPANISH	muro
FRENCH	mur

They have all taken their word from *murus*, a more general Latin word for *wall*. If you don't like English being the odd one out, think about what we call a picture which is painted on a wall.

FOR THE NEXT TEN MINUTES SUPERBRAIN WORKS HARD...

NGAAUUHHH! PUFF! PANT!

...PROPPING UP SHATTERED WALLS

...SAVING MEN, WOMEN AND CHILDREN TRAPPED INSIDE COLLAPSED BUILDINGS.....

WHY DO I DO THIS?!

TO SAVE

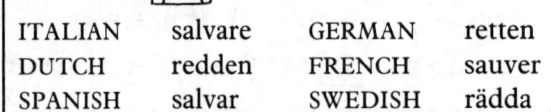

ITALIAN	salvare	GERMAN	retten
DUTCH	redden	FRENCH	sauver
SPANISH	salvar	SWEDISH	rädda

Here English has taken the Romance word and not the Germanic one. We also have *safe*, *saviour* and *salvation*. Some people rescue abandoned ships or their cargo, and then sell them. What do you call their business?

TEN 📼

DUTCH	tien	ITALIAN	dieci
GERMAN	zehn	SPANISH	diez
SWEDISH	tio	FRENCH	dix

Ten can also be traced further:

LATIN	decem	RUSSIAN	desját'
WELSH	deg	GREEK	deca
BENGALI	dosh		

TREE 📼

DUTCH	boom
GERMAN	Baum
SWEDISH	träd
ITALIAN	albero
SPANISH	árbol
FRENCH	arbre

English *tree* is clearly close to the Swedish. But what do you call a long length of wood used in house building or in gymnastics? We have also taken words from the Romance languages. What is arboriculture? What are arboreal animals?

📼

HOSPITAL The Italians call it an *ospedale*; in Spain it's an *hospital*, and in France an *hôpital*. The Dutch call it *ziekenhuis*. What does *ziek* mean? The Germans say *Krankenhaus*, so if you are *ziek* in the Netherlands you are *krank* in Germany. What is a *Krankenwagen* and a *Krankenschwester*? Where might you feel *seekrank*?

CHILD 📼

DUTCH	kind	ITALIAN	ragazza/o
GERMAN	Kind	SPANISH	niño/niña
SWEDISH	barn	FRENCH	enfant

A variety of words, and not one of them like our word *child*. What is a popular word for *child* in Scotland and North East England (where Vikings once settled)? What English word for a young child is related to the French *enfant*?

14 Last but not least

In this book you have looked mainly at six European languages. But what about the other European languages? Look at the map below.

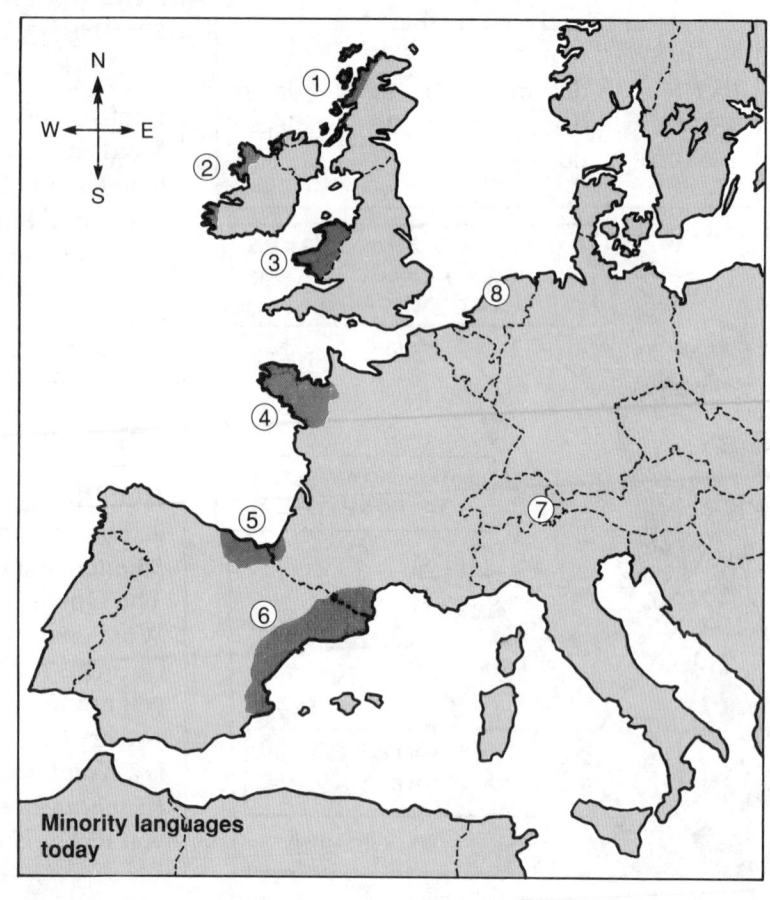

Minority languages today

FRISIAN: a Germanic language very like Dutch. 400,000 speakers.

ROMANSH: Romance language developed from Latin. Spoken by 30,000 Swiss people.

CATALAN: Romance language developed from Latin. Spoken in eastern Spain by 5 million people.

BASQUE: an ancient language, unrelated to any other. Spoken by 500,000 in Spain, and by 70,000 more over the border in France.

WELSH – 600,000 speakers.
SCOTS GAELIC – 75,000.
IRISH GAELIC (ERSE) – 500,000.
Celtic languages spoken along the western edge of English-speaking countries. The Celts were pushed westwards by the Anglo-Saxons.

BRETON: the Celtic language of France, taken there by the Celtic speakers of Cornwall. The last native Cornish-speaker died in 1777.

Can you match up the languages with the numbered areas on the map.

These languages are called MINORITY LANGUAGES. Minority languages are languages spoken by a minority in a particular country. *Some* minority languages were once more powerful and widespread, but are now under pressure from neighbouring languages. Also under pressure are the special ways of living and thinking which minority-language-speakers often have.

Find Iceland in your atlas. Icelandic, spoken by only 240,000 people, is never called a minority language. Welsh, spoken in parts of Wales certainly is a minority language, even though it has twice as many speakers as Icelandic. What's the difference?

These days Welsh is taught in Welsh schools, along with English. It was not always so. In the 19th and early 20th centuries schoolchildren were punished for speaking Welsh. This has often been the case with minority languages. In Brittany teachers once put up notices saying 'NO SPITTING. NO SPEAKING BRETON!'

> Minority languages. Why bother to keep them all going? Those who speak them always learn English anyway – just to keep in touch with the rest of the world. And if a minority language starts losing speakers, that's because it's a pretty boring and feeble language in the first place.

Discuss Superbrain's arguments, using what you have learnt in this book, and work out some replies.

From the author

On the first page you read that this book was about the English you use every day, and about how it is related to other languages spoken in Europe. Now that you have looked at (and listened to) some neighbouring languages, I hope that you will look at your own language – as well as any foreign language that you study, or that your schoolfriends speak – with more interest and curiosity.

Jim McGurn

Acknowledgements

Maps by Andrew Wilson
Cartoons and cover illustration
by Elivia Savadier